T0195826

Grades
5–8

OPEN
FOR BUSINESS
A Simulation for Student-Run Enterprises

Written by Cindy Slovacek
Illustrated by Elisa Ahlin

First published 2005 by Prufrock Press Inc.

Published 2021 by Routledge
605 Third Avenue, New York, NY 10017
2 Park Square, Milton Park, Abingdon, Oxon OX14 4RN

Routledge is an imprint of the Taylor & Francis Group, an informa business

ISBN 13: 978-1-59363-115-4 (pbk)

Dedication
This book is dedicated to Ronnie, Amber, and Megan for their constant love and support.

Edited by Dianne Draze and Zoe Saba

NEW YORK AND LONDON

Contents

Information for the Instructor

About This Unit

This unit was developed to give upper inter-mediate and junior high students an introduction to owning and running a business. During the course of the unit, students will divide into groups (businesses) that will make a product and sell it to other students on campus. Through this proce-dure students will be introduced to many facets of business ownership including deciding on a prod-uct to produce, planning for materials and facili-ties, securing capital, selecting a favorable location, creating advertising, bookkeeping, and practicing sales techniques. As they work together in their groups, they will be building skills in coop-eration, compromise, decision making, and prob-lem solving.

The teacher's role in this unit is to be a facili-tator. After a few introductory lessons and discus-sions, students break into their groups and begin planning their businesses. Your role is to guide their decisions, answer their questions, and make sure they work on a time line that will allow them to be ready to sell their products on the two sale days you have arranged.

Teacher's Information

This book is divided into two main sections. The first section is for the instructor. In this section, everything that must be done, both by the teacher and by the student groups, is outlined. This is so that you have a guideline of what students need to do, the order in which each task should be completed, a list of your responsibilities, and les-sons or class discussions you will want to interject. Each direction is coded so you will know whether it pertains to a whole-class activity, is an explana-tion of what the student groups should do, is infor-mation for you, or is a reminder of something you need to do. The symbols that are used are:

    📁   information for the instructor

    ☞   action item for the instructor

    〰   whole-class activity

    ❖   small student group activity

Student Section

The student section of this book includes an outline of everything they will need to think about or do to make their business a reality. This section also includes all the forms they will need to com-plete for planning purposes and to enter into agreements for rentals or loans. You will probably want to duplicate these forms beforehand and give them to each group in a folder, so they can work on each phase of the project at their own pace.

Student Objectives

By completing this simulation students will be able to:

- describe and apply the techniques used in effective advertisements
- define common economic terms and use the terms in conversation
- identify factors that are necessary for a suc-cessful business
- understand how competition relates to the production of a product
- identify factors that influence economic de-cisions involved in operating a busines (lo-cation, prices, types of products, cost of raw materials, etc.)
- describe consumer decision-making factors when purchasing a product
- recognize the value of compromise
- use decision-making skills
- use problem-solving skills

Sequence of Lessons and Activities

1. Prior to Starting

📁 **Approval** - You will need to get approval for this project from your principal because all students on campus will be involved in the sale of merchandise. You should plan to keep the money for your students in a secure place between classes. Make arrangements for where you will keep the money before you introduce this unit. You should also check on any requirements for collecting and reporting sales tax.

📁 **Guest Speakers** - At some point during this unit, you may wish to invite in one or more speakers to discuss some of the various aspects of this unit. You might consider inviting a small business owner (either a retailer or a manufacturer or both), an accountant, a bank officer, someone who owns an advertising business, or someone from your chamber of commerce. Speakers could make presentations at any point during the unit.

2. Class Introduction

〰 **Class Discussion** - As a group, think of various businesses in your town. Have students give reasons why they like certain businesses or reasons they think particular businesses are successful. List these ideas on the chalkboard or on a transparency. Ideas might include quality of products, prices, location, a good selection of products, or service. Have students discuss what a business must consider to stay in business and be successful.

Briefly describe the unit. Explain that students will be dividing into groups, and each group will be a business that will manufacture a product (food, drink, or some nonedible item) and sell the product to the other students on campus. They will do all the planning and financial transactions that a real business would do.

3. Role Play Activity

Materials: Name cards for the roles listed on page 13, play money

〰 **Class Activity** - Lead students through the role play as described on page 13.

4. Vocabulary Activity

Materials: *Business Vocabulary* worksheet

〰 **Class Activity** - Have students complete the vocabulary worksheet on page 14. Discuss the terms, their definitions, and how they relate to the role playing activity that students just completed.

5. Types of Businesses and Ownership

Materials: *Types of Businesses* worksheet

📁 Before students actually begin their businesses, they should know that there are several different types of business and three basic types of business ownership. Businesses are typically divided into three categories:

- **Manufacturers** - This business produces products. While they can sell the products directly to the consumer, they typically sell to distributors and other retailers who buy in larger quantities at wholesale prices and then resell the products to the ultimate consumers.
- **Retailers** - These business owners usually do not manufacture the goods they sell. They buy products at a discount from manufacturers and resell them at a profit.
- **Services** - These businesses provide services rather than products.

Explain that sometimes businesses fall into more than one category. A service business, like a beauty shop, may sell products in addition to offering their services; while some services, like an advertising firm or a bike repair shop, would probably just provide a service. A retailer, like an art gallery, might also sell some of the paintings that the owner produced. A bakery could be just a manufacturer and sell their products through other stores or it could sell their baked goods through their own retail store.

〰 **Class Activity** - Have students complete the worksheet entitled *Types of Businesses* found on page 15. After they have finished, discuss their examples.

📁 You may want to introduce your class to the three types of business ownership, though this is optional. The three main types of ownership are:

- **Sole Proprietorship** - These businesses are owned and operated by one person (plus any employees they may hire). It is the most wide-spread form of small business ownership.
- **Partnership** - These businesses are owned by two or more people who are co-owners of a business. In most cases they share the expenses, the work, and the profits from the business.
- **Corporation** - A corporation is an association of individuals created by law and existing as an entity with powers and liabilities independent of its members. Legal papers must be filed with the state in which a business operates before it can become a corporation. Most businesses do not begin as corporations. Sole proprietorships and partnerships may eventually change the ownership to a corporation because of legal or economic reasons or because they want to raise capital by selling shares of the business.

≋ **Class Discussion** - (Optional) You may want to discuss these three types of ownership. If so, have students as a group think of advantages and disadvantages of each type of ownership.

6. Assign Groups

≋ Divide the class into groups and assign two managers for each group. The number of groups (businesses) and number of members in each group will vary depending on your class and school size. Explain that each group will own its own business and share in any profits made or losses incurred. The business will sell for two days (30 minutes each day) to their market, the students on campus. If a student does not cooperate or causes trouble for his or her group, the managers and the teacher can create an improvement plan. If this plan is not followed, the student can be removed from the business and will lose all claims to any profits.

7. Distribute Folders

📁 Assemble folders with all the information and forms from pages 16 through 29 and distribute these to each group. These folders should stay in the classroom.

Students should work on completing these forms with your guidance. While they may work at their own pace, you may wish to set some deadlines so the unit is not drawn out too long. The "Steps to a Successful Business" gives students an outline of the things they will need to do and the sequence that should be followed.

The rest of this section gives you, the instructor, an outline of the steps that should be followed, including things students need to do, things you need to do, and instructions or guidelines you will need to give them. There are more details and instructions in this section, so you will want to read all the instructions carefully so you can give students any additional information that you deem necessary.

8. Begin Business Planning

Materials: *Beginning Your Business* worksheet

❖ **Organize Groups** - Have students decide what product they will produce and sell and what they will call their business using the *Beginning Your Business* worksheet. Group members should exchange phone numbers in case they need to contact each other outside of school. Students should get your approval before doing anything else.

9. Bookkeeping

Materials: *Transaction Record* transparency, *Transaction Record*, a copy for each group.

≋ **Guided Practice** - Make a transparency of the *Transaction Record* and demonstrate how students will record expenses and income.

Explain that they will be recording every expense (purchases of raw materials for making the product, rent for space, equipment, utilities, and advertising) throughout the unit. Every time they incur an expense or sign an agreement, they will attach the receipt or agreement to the *Transaction Record*. Explain that some of their bills, like raw materials, will be paid as they are incurred, while others (rentals, repayment of the loan) will be paid after the sale.

Give each person a copy of the form and have them practice by recording several entries for a hypothetical business that you dictate to them.

10. Sources of Capital

☷ **Class Discussion** - Students will want to know early on how they will finance their project, so it is worth taking a class period at this point to discuss financing in general and the financing of this project in particular.

Discuss the fact that a business will need **capital**, money to start the business. Brainstorm why businesses need capital. Ask, "What do you have to pay?" Then brainstorm sources of capital. Answers may include entrepreneur's own savings, loans from friends or relatives, loans from a bank, or selling shares of ownership. Distinguish the difference between private ownership (a sole proprietor or partners) and a corporation (ownership by a group of share holders). When a business incorporates, the shares can be owned solely by an individual or by a group of owners. The people who own shares in the business do not need to be involved with the day-to-day workings of the business. In most small businesses, such as the ones the students are starting, whether the business is incorporated or not, the capital comes from the owners or from loans.

Discuss the risks and benefits of the business owner investing his or her own money. By investing their own money, owners have no interest to pay; but, on the other hand, they may lose all of their money.

Interest is the major source of income for banks today. For this reason, loans are only made to qualified people who can guarantee to repay the loan with interest. Entrepreneurs must convince lenders they can repay the loan by offering as much information as possible about the endeavor and, in many cases, sufficient **collateral**. Banks are often reluctant to loan money to individuals who do not have an established business record and some assets. Also, most banks will often insist that owners invest some of their own money so that the owners have a vested interest in the success of their business. A bank will not usually give a loan for 100% of the funds that are needed to start a new business.

For this unit students will get the funds they need to make their product, advertise, and cover rental fees by contributing some of the funds jointly and getting a loan from an agreeable adult for the remainder. The group may only invest up to two-thirds of the total capital. A loan must be secured for the additional amount of capital that is needed. The specifics of determining the amount of money they will need and from whom they could get a loan comes later in the unit, after they have determined all their expenses.

11. Business Location

Materials: *Rental Agreement,* poster board

☷ **Class Discussion** - Discuss the fact that traditionally businesses were established where demand clearly existed or near the raw materials that were needed to make their products. With modern forms of communication and transportation, many businesses are now established in locations that are not near the raw materials needed or the intended consumers.

Ask students to provide examples from their experiences of stores in your town that are located close to their customers (copy services and Laundromats close to colleges, restaurants close to tourist attractions, bait shops close to fishing facilities, etc.). Also ask for examples of businesses that are located close to the sources of their raw materials or labor supply (a fresh fish store close to the waterfront, a cement manufacturer close to a sand or rock quarry, a petroleum refinery close to an oil pipeline, a manufacturer of plywood close to a source of timber, or a clothing manufacturer close to a source of inexpensive labor).

Discuss the difference between desirable locations for a retail business, a manufacturing firm, and someone who offers a service.

In retail businesses, location is very important. Often the money that is saved by renting a store in a less desirable location is needed for advertising to draw customers to the less desirable location. For retail businesses that specialize in providing goods to customers in their own towns, the owners must consider how their location will make them more accessible or less accessible to their customers. Another consideration, however, is the rental price. The most desirable, accessible locations will usually cost more to rent.

As a class, discuss locations on campus where the student businesses could locate. List the locations on the board or on a large piece of paper.

☞ **Post Rental Prices** - After the students have made a list of campus locations, you may select the most appropriate locations that do not interfere with other activities and make a list of locations and rental prices. Base your decisions about rental prices on:

- nearness to facilities (electricity and water)
- a pleasant environment in which to work
- accessibility to consumers.

The price also includes one poster board to display at the business on which groups can list their products and prices. A sample of rental prices for the two sale days might look like the following:

far end of the football field	.10
cafeteria	1.40
courtyard	1.20
hallway by bathrooms	.90
playground near the cafeteria	.20
front sidewalk	.80
bleachers at the baseball field	.05

Remember that you want the students to make a profit, so keep the rental prices low, between five cents and $1.50. If other rooms are to be used, get the approval of the person in charge of that room. Any rent that is collected from the businesses using this area would then be paid to that individual or to the school's general fund. Decide beforehand with your principal whether the money that is collected for rent should be donated to the school or used as some reward for your class.

☞ Make a poster listing locations and rental prices.

❖ **Select Locations** - Students should review the list of rental prices after you have posted it and discuss the advantages and disadvantages of each site. Before they decide on a location, discuss these questions:

- Which site would have the most customers passing by who would be interested in buying your product?
- Is the site accessible to customers?
- Does the site have the facilities (heat, shade, electricity, lighting, fresh air, etc.) that you need?
- Is the price fair and affordable?
- Are there any other positive or negative aspects of the sites on the list?

All sites should be available on a first-come, first-serve basis. Students should check with you to make sure the site they want is available before filling out the rental agreement. Once their selection has been reserved, they should complete the *Rental Agreement*, giving you one copy and keeping one copy with their transaction record.

12. Planning Equipment and Utilities
Materials: *Equipment and Utilities Planning* and *Equipment and Utilities Rental Agreement*

❖ **List Equipment Needs** -Students should list all the equipment they will need on the *Equipment Planning* sheet. They should include tables, chairs, spoons, bowls, ice chests, heating units, glue guns, computers, or anything needed to make their product. They should then check with each other and with other people to see where they can get these items and how much they will have to pay.

❖ **List Rental Prices** - If students have several sources for a piece of equipment, they should note the rental price from each source. A list of the equipment, the sources for each item of equipment, and the rental prices should be put on the bottom of the *Equipment Planning* sheet.

❖ **Fill Out the Rental Agreement** - Students should fill out a *Rental Agreement* for each item they will rent and list the rental costs on their *Transaction Record* as an expense. One copy of each agreement stays with the group's records and one goes to the person who is renting the equipment to them. Have more copies of the *Rental Agreement* forms available if students need them.

❖ **Arrange for Utilities** - Students should then decide what utilities (water, electricity), if any, they will need. If they need utilities, they should fill out a *Rental Agreement*, keep one copy and attach it to their *Transaction Record* and give one copy to the person from whom they are leasing the utility. They should then add this expense to their *Transaction Record*.

13. Planning for Raw Materials

Materials: *Raw Materials Planning* sheet and *Purchase Order*

❖ **Listing Materials** - The raw materials are the ingredients or materials students will need to make their products. They should list all the needed raw materials on the *Raw Materials Planning* sheet.

❖ **Check Prices** - Students should then check the prices of these ingredients or materials at several stores, comparing several different brands of each product and recording the prices on the *Raw Materials Planning* sheet. After they have a list of prices, they should as a group decide where they will purchase their materials.

❖ **Decide on Needed Amounts** - The next step is to decide on the amount of each ingredient or material they will need. On the *Purchase Order* they should record the amount of each item they will be buying, the place where they will buy it, the price they expect to pay, and which group member will purchase each item.

❖ **Paying for the Purchases** - As a group, students need to decide how they will pay for their purchases. They can either use money from the loan they will take out or they can have the person who will be buying the material pay for it and then reimburse this person after they have sold their products.

14. Planning Advertisements

Materials: *Advertising Rates, Advertising Agreement*

📁 **Advertising Options** - You may offer students two advertising opportunities - posters and live performances that they can perform in other classrooms with permission from the teacher. You should fill in the prices for posters and live performances before distributing the *Advertising Rates* to each group.

Students may want to combine groups to save advertising money. This is acceptable since the audience count is irrelevant. They are being charged for the time they are using in a classroom or the space they are using by posting a poster. You may suggest that they combine their efforts or you may want to approve this idea only if they suggest it.

If students want to make fliers in addition to the posters, charge them the cost of duplicating the fliers and set a fee like five cents per copy. They may wish to go to a copying service where they can get a greater variety of paper selections, or they may wish to create fliers on their computers. Students should come up with the idea to make fliers themselves. Part of being a good business person is creativity, so you don't want to give them all the suggestions.

〰 **Group Discussion** - Ask students to pay close attention to advertisements on television and radio, in newspapers and magazines, noting which are most effective. Have them bring in several good examples. As a class, make a list of several different advertising techniques and discuss why they are effective and what audience they appeal to. Review the information on advertising under Planning Your Advertising on the *Advertising Rate* sheet. Discuss how these techniques were used in the examples you collected.

❖ **Planning Advertisements** - Instruct each group to discuss what things they want to include in their ads. They should consider the following:

- business name
- location
- dates and times of operation
- products they will be selling
- catchy slogans
- incentives or special offers that would induce people to come to the business or buy more products (reduced prices, prizes, special sales)
- reasons why people should buy what they are selling

Students should consult the *Advertisement Rates* sheet for the cost of various print and live advertisements and then decide what kind of advertisement their group wants to produce. If they are going to make posters, they should decide how many posters, the size of the posters, the information they want to include, and the design they will use. Encourage them to sketch out several ideas before they decide on the best one(s).

❖ **Purchasing Advertisement** - After planning, students need to come to you and make arrangements for their poster advertising by completing and signing copies of the *Advertising Agreement*. They should then add this expense to their *Transaction Record*, attach a copy of the agreement to the expense record, and give you one copy.

☞ Keep a list of each business's ads. Check off the ads as they are posted and collect payment after the sale. Have students turn in each flyer after the sale to ensure that all ads have been removed from the campus. A penalty could be charged for any flyers that are not removed.

15. Creating Advertisements

Materials: various sizes of poster board, colored markers or paint

❖ **Make the Advertisements** - After planning, students then make their posters and create their skits if they choose to perform live commercials. They do not show the prices for their products on the posters; a separate poster should be made and displayed at their booths for this purpose. Remind them to check their spelling and make the posters as neatly as possible.

☞❖ **Posting the Advertisements** - Inform students when and where they can post the advertisements.

16. Securing Loans

Materials: *Loan Application*, and *Loan Agreement*

📁 At this point, students should have all the information they need to determine how much money they will need to make their product, advertise to their potential customers, and rent the facilities and utilities they need to sell the product. They now need to complete an application for a loan, select several people who they think might give them a loan, and approach each of these people with their applications to request a loan.

〰 **Class Discussion** - Review with students that interest is the money a bank charges for use of its money. Interest is calculated by multiplying the principal (amount of money borrowed) times the rate times the time for which the money is borrowed.

$$I = P \times R \times T$$

In real-life transactions, the time is one year or some fraction or multiple of one year. Interest on $100 at a rate of 10% would be the following amounts for the times given:

1 month	$ .83
6 months	$5.00
1 year	$10.00
2 years	$20.00

For ease of calculations and record keeping, for this simulation you may choose to calculate the interest as if the entire time for which the loan is taken out is one year rather than a fraction of a year.

❖ **Determining Loans Amounts** - To determine how much of a loan they will need, each group should first decide if any of the partners want to invest their own money in the business. The group may only invest up to two-thirds of the total capital that they will need. A loan must be used to cover the difference between what the partners invest and the total that is needed to cover expenses.

❖ **Determining Collateral** - The partners should discuss what collateral they would be willing to offer in exchange for a loan. They may offer tangible items or promises to complete a certain amount of work. All members must put up an equal amount of collateral (items of equal value or a promise to do an equal amount of work). Stress that if the loan cannot be repaid, collection of the collateral will be made.

❖ **Filling Out the Loan Application** - Each group will then fill out a loan application. To do this, they will need to determine what they will charge for their product. For this, they will need to consider the cost of producing the product (raw materials plus any items they will need to rent) as well as what their customers would be willing to pay.

❖ **Applying for a Loan** - Each group should brainstorm where their business could get a loan. After they have made a list of several different sources, they should choose one adult (teacher, parent, principal) to ask for the loan. They should take the *Loan Application* to the person who they would like to ask for a loan, having first considered what questions the person may ask and being prepared to answer the questions.

If the person does not approve the group's loan for a rate of interest that they find acceptable (10% is an acceptable rate), they can choose another source and repeat the process. If approved, they should sign the *Loan Agreement*, keep one copy, and give the person from whom they received the loan the other copy. The money should be given to you for safe keeping until they need to withdraw some for expenses. They should record the amount as income on their *Transaction Record*.

17. Pre-Sale Activities

≋ **Class Discussion** - Hold a class discussion about how to handle customers, how to count change, how to make sure food is handled in a sanitary fashion, what problems might arise, and what strategies might be used to prevent or deal with these problems. You might suggest that they decide beforehand what jobs need to be done and who will do them. The person who is handling the food should not handle the money.

☞ **Inform Other Classes and Parents** Ask other teachers on your staff to discuss with their students how to be good consumers. Try to encourage students to look at what each business is selling before purchasing anything.

One week prior to the sale, send a letter home with all students on campus that will be involved as consumers. This letter should simply explain the project and ask for students to bring money on the sale days if they wish to purchase the products that will be offered.

❖ **Make Price Signs** - Each group should make a sign that lists their company's name, their products and prices, and any special offers. If they want to decorate their sales booth in any additional way, they should make the decorations.

18. Make the Product

❖ Each group should purchase the raw materials they will need and make the products.

19. Sale Dates

☞ **Set Dates** - Select two days for students to sell their products. These days may be consecutive or you may skip a day between the sales.

❖ **Get Change** - Students will need to get five dollars in change. They can get it by taking five dollars from their capital account and getting change from a bank or they may choose to have one partner contribute the change (if so, it should

be entered as an expense and will need to be repaid after the sale).

❖ **Day One Selling** - On the day of the sale, they will set up their sales stations and sell for 30 minutes. Afterward, they should clean up and as a group make decisions about the next sale day. They should decide:
- Are more materials needed? If so, what kind and how much?
- Did some things sell better than other things?
- If more materials are needed, who will purchase them?
- Do they need to change their prices?
- What other problems need to be addressed?

They may not add new products, but they may choose to discontinue products that did not sell well or products with a low profit margin. Remind them that they want to make a profit. The loan must be repaid, and a profit is desirable.

❖ ☞ **Count Money** - They should count their money and give it to you for safekeeping.

❖ **Day Two Selling** - On the second sale day, each group should again set up a sales station and sell their products. When they are finished, they need to clean up. If they have leftovers, they need to decide what to do with them. If possible, they should find a market for them. They may have to sell them at discounted prices or try to sell them to an adult. It is not wise to just distribute the remaining products among the partners because that is lost profit.

❖ **Clean Up** - Have students remove all advertisements that are still posted around the campus and turn in each poster to you.

20. After the Sale
Materials - envelopes

❖ **Settle Debts** - After the two sale days, students will count their money, pay their debts (including the loan plus interest) and record their expenses and incomes. They should pay their debts using the envelopes that you will provide. They should give an envelope with the correct amount of money to each person to whom they owe money. On the front of the envelope, they will write the person's name and the amount they are paying this person, seal the envelope, and deliver each envelope to the person for whom it is intended. They should get a receipt to prove that the money was repaid to the person(s) who made the loan(s). They will also need to repay the five dollars in change if they got it from any funds other than their business funds and repay the investment each partner made.

❖ **Record Keeping** - At this point, they should check to see that all expenses have been entered on their *Transaction Record*.

21. Figuring Profit

〜 **Class Discussion** - Explain that profit is the amount of money left over after a business has paid all expenses and repaid any loans. The amount of cash each business has retained should be the same as the profit that is shown on the transaction record after subtracting all expenses from the income. Divide the total profit by the number of partners to determine the profit per person.

❖ **Reporting Profit** - Ask each group to turn in a sheet with the following information:
- Business name
- Names of the partners
- Products that were sold
- Total profit
- Profit per person

📁 Depending on what you have decided beforehand, you may let students divide up their profits, donate the profits to a good cause, or buy something for the class with the money.

22. Evaluation

Materials - paper

〜 **Class Discussion** - Evaluate how the various businesses fared. Why did some businesses make more money than others? What problems arose and how were they solved? What problems might arise in a real business? What makes a successful business?

〜 **Listing Activity** - Write the following assignment on the board or on a transparency. Ask

students to write the answers to each question, then share their lists with a partner, and then share the lists with the entire class.
- List five things you learned from this unit
- List four necessities to operate a successful business
- List three problems faced in business
- List two advantages of owning your own business
- List one disadvantage of owning your own business

〜 **Class Discussion** - Seat students in a large circle of desks or chairs. Ask each student to respond to the following:
- The purpose of this unit was . . .
- I learned that . . .
- I feel that . . .

〜 **Test** - Administer test on pages 30 - 31. You may also choose to grade each student group's worksheets.

23. Thank Yous

〜 Have students write thank you letters to parents or others who helped them. Deliver the letters. A sample of a letter to parents might look like the following:

Dear Parents,
We would like to thank you for your cooperation in making our business a success. Our business would not have been profitable without your advice, transportation, dedication, and help. We appreciate the opportunity to participate in this learning activity and experience what it is like to own a small business. Every business was able to show a profit. We learned many things during our time as entrepreneurs. Thank you again for your support.
Sincerely,

Students may also create their own letters. This would be more personal and meaningful.

Entrepreneur Role-Play Activity

1. Introduce the situation that an entrepreneur wants to start his or her own business. Assign the following roles to students.

owner/entrepreneur	loan officer
accountant	landlord
supplier	worker 1
worker 2	worker 3
radio station manager	TV executive
newspaper advertising manager	
consumer 1	consumer 2
consumer 3	consumer 4
consumer 5	

   You will trace the actions of a person who is starting a business. As you read the following scenarios, students should act out the scene.

2. Have students list possible expenses that may be associated with starting this new business.

3. The owner needs money to start this business. The owner, therefore, goes to the loan officer of the local bank and requests to borrow $200. This is the **capital** needed to begin the business.

4. The loan officer is taking a risk that the business will be successful and that the loan will be repaid. Discuss **interest**, the fee the bank charges to use its money for a certain amount of time. Then ask, "How do you compensate the bank if the business is unsuccessful and the loan cannot be repaid?" Discuss **collateral**, something the owner will put up as a guarantee that the loan will be repaid. Students should role play the questions the loan officer and the owner need to ask; for instance, the type of collateral that is needed, the amount of interest, the date the loan should be repaid, whether the owner has a good plan for making a profit, whether the amount of the loan is sufficient to cover all expenses, and if all requests are reasonable.

5. When the loan officer and the owner agree on the terms of the loan, the loan is approved. The owner receives $200. Give the owner play money in various denominations.

6. The owner leases a building from the landlord for $40. Forty dollars is given to the landlord.

7. The accountant keeps a record of the business's income and expenses on the chalkboard as money is spent or earned. At this point, have the accountant record the following:

Transaction	Amount	Balance
loan	$200	$200
rent	$40	$160

8. The owner must buy raw materials from the supplier. Sixty dollars is given to the supplier. The accountant records this on the list of expenses and income under expense. The balance should now be $120.

9. The owner hires three workers (**labor**) for $20 per day to produce the product he or she plans to manufacture. Each worker is given $20 and the accountant records the expenses.

10. The owner contacts the radio station manager, the newspaper advertising manager, and the television executive about prices to advertise the product in the various media. The radio station charges $20, the newspaper charges $10, and a commercial on television is $40. Each student representing the three media should try to sell his or her advertising medium, stating benefits of advertising in the particular medium. The owner should choose one form of advertising. The appropriate amount of money should be given to that person and the expense should be recorded.

11. The owner sells the products to the various consumers. Each of the five consumers buys $60 worth of products. The consumers give the owner $60 each and the accountant records an income of $300 and the corresponding balance (this will vary depending on the type of advertising that was chosen). The money that is remaining after all the expenses have been paid is the **profit**. The owner may keep this amount in the business to pay for more raw materials and advertising or to finance expansion of the business into new products or new markets. The owner will usually need to take some of the profit for his or her own wage. Depending on the amount of profit and the nature of the business, the owner may also share some of the profit with the workers (profit sharing), thus providing an incentive for working efficiently and producing a good product as economically as possible.

Business Vocabulary

Name _____

Write a definition for each of the following terms.

boycott _____

budget _____

capital _____

capitalism _____

collateral _____

consumer _____

entrepreneur_____

expenses _____

free enterprise system _____

income _____

interest _____

labor _____

lease _____

loan _____

market _____

monopoly _____

profit _____

raw materials _____

rent _____

_____

retail _____

_____

Types of Businesses

Name: _____

Here are definitions of the three main types of businesses. For each one, give three examples of businesses in your community whose main type of work would fit the definition.

Manufacturers

These businesses manufacturer products that they sell wholesale (in large quantities and at a discount) to retailers or in some cases directly to their customers.

Retailers

These businesses usually do not manufacture goods. They buy their products from manufacturers and resell them to the consumers at a profit.

Services

These businesses provide services (skills and time of the people who work in the business) to their customers rather than products.

_____

_____

_____

What are two businesses in your community that could fall into more than one of these categories?

_____

_____

Steps to a Successful Business

The following is a list of everything your group will do in this unit on starting your own business. Any forms you will need are included in your folder. As you complete each step, check it off.

Planning Your Business

- ☐ Decide on a product
- ☐ Decide on a business name
- ☐ Fill out the Beginning Your Business form

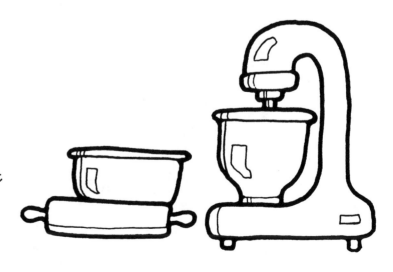

Start Bookkeeping

- ☐ Put the Transaction Record in a prominent place in your folder
- ☐ Record all expenses and income as they are incurred
- ☐ Attach copies of all receipts and agreements

Locating Your Business

- ☐ Check rental prices
- ☐ Discuss what location would be best for your business
- ☐ Decide on a location
- ☐ Check to make sure the location is available
- ☐ Sign the rental agreement

Planning for Equipment and Utilities

- ☐ List the equipment you will need
- ☐ Find out where you can rent each item and how much it will cost to rent
- ☐ Decide what utilities you will need
- ☐ Complete a rental agreement for each piece of equipment and utility you will need to rent

Planning for Raw Materials

☐ List the ingredients or materials you will need
☐ Check prices for each item
☐ Determine quantities for each item
☐ Fill out a purchase order
☐ Decide how you will pay for your purchases

Planning Your Advertising

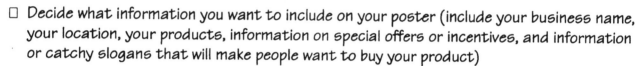

☐ Become aware of advertising techniques used on television, radio and in magazines
☐ Check the price list for advertising
☐ Decide what kinds of posters and how many of each one you want to make
☐ Decide what information you want to include on your poster (include your business name, your location, your products, information on special offers or incentives, and information or catchy slogans that will make people want to buy your product)
☐ If you want to do a skit to advertise your product, get permission from the teachers
☐ Complete the Advertising Agreement

Creating Your Advertisements

☐ Make your posters
☐ Post your posters
☐ If you are doing live commercials, write, practice and perform your live commercials in other rooms

Securing a Loan

☐ Determine how much money you will need
☐ Decide how much the partners will invest
☐ Decide what you will offer as collateral
☐ Make a list of people from whom you can get a loan
☐ Fill out the loan application
☐ Apply for the loan
☐ Record the amount on your transaction record

Before the Sale

- ☐ Post advertisements and do live commercials
- ☐ Determine prices
- ☐ Make a poster listing your products, prices, and any special offers
- ☐ Get $5.00 in change
- ☐ Plan your sales – draw a plan of the sales booth and assign jobs for each person
- ☐ Bring a box for your supplies the day of the sale

Make Your Product

- ☐ Purchase supplies
- ☐ Make your product
- ☐ Record your expenses on your transaction record

The Sale

- ☐ Set up your sales space
- ☐ Sell your product
- ☐ Evaluate how the first day's sale went
- ☐ Make any adjustments that are needed for the second sales day

After the Sale

- ☐ Clean Up
- ☐ Count your money

Settle Your Debts

- ☐ Pay any debts
- ☐ Repay the loan plus interest
- ☐ Repay each partner for his or her investment
- ☐ Repay the $5.00 in change if it did not come from your business's funds
- ☐ Make sure all expenses have been entered on your transaction record and all receipts and agreements have been attached
- ☐ Figure your profit
- ☐ Report your profit to your teacher

Beginning Your Business

Company Name _____

Each business will produce and sell some type of product, food, or drink. With your group, make a list of possible products. List all your ideas.

Product Ideas

_____   _____

_____   _____

_____   _____

_____   _____

_____   _____

_____   _____

_____   _____

As you decide which product your business will make, you will need to consider the cost of the raw materials needed to make the product, the market, whether it is something the consumers want or need, and the competition. Once you have decided on a product (or several products) you want to produce and sell, you must get approval from the teacher.

The product(s) we will sell _____

_____

The name of our business _____

_____

Partners _____   _____

_____   _____

_____   _____

Approved by

_____
     teacher

Transaction Record

Company Name _____

Amount	Expenses			Income			Balance
	Paid to	Reason for payment	✓ when paid	Amount	Source		

Rental Agreement
Sales Location

The company of _____ agrees to pay

$_____ to _____ for the use of

_____ for thirty (30) minutes on two days on

the dates of _____ and _____. We agree to leave

the rented space clean and suitable for use at the end of each business day. We also agree

that the following penalties could be enforced by the teacher or the owner of the site:

- $5.00 for the area left unclean
- $3.00 for disciplinary action (horseplay, endangering other students, damaging the site, etc.)

This agreement is signed on _____ (date) and agreed to by all parties

whose signature appears below.

_____
owner of sales location

Partners

_____

_____

_____

_____

_____

Equipment Planning

Business Name _____

List all the equipment that you will need. For each item, list a couple of different sources and the rental price for each source.

Equipment to be rented	Source	Price

Final Decision on Rentals

List all the equipment you will rent, the person from whom you will rent each item and the price you will pay. Then complete a Rental Agreement for each person from whom you will rent equipment. Attach a copy of these agreements to your Transaction Record and enter the amounts as expenses on the Transaction Record.

Equipment	Source	Price

Rental Agreement
Equipment and Utilities

The company of _____ agrees to rent _____

_____ from _____ for the

amount of $_____. The rental will be for the period of time between

_____ and _____. The rental amount will

be paid in full after the use of the equipment or utility.

Owner of equipment or utility   date

_____   _____

Partners _____   _____

_____   _____

_____   _____

Rental Agreement
Equipment and Utilities

The company of _____ agrees to rent _____

_____ from _____ for the

amount of $_____. The rental will be for the period of time between

_____ and _____. The rental amount will be

paid in full after the use of the equipment or utility.

Owner of equipment or utility   date

_____   _____

Partners _____   _____

_____   _____

_____   _____

Raw Materials Planning

Company Name_____

List all the materials you will need to make your
product. For each item check the price of several
different brands at several different stores.

Materials Needed	Store	Brand	Price

Purchase Order
Raw Materials and Ingredients

Company Name _____

List all the materials your business will need to buy to make their product, the amount of each item you will purchase, where the items will be purchased, and who will be responsible for making the purchases.

Raw Materials Needed	Quantity	Source	Buyer

Remember to keep all the receipts. Attach them to the Transaction Record and record them as expenses.

Advertisement Rates

Posters

Black and White

Prices

up to 9" x 12" (small sheet of construction paper)   _____

9" x 12" to 14" x 22" (1/2 a poster board)   _____

14" x 22" to 28" x 22" (1 poster board)   _____

larger than 28" x 22"   _____

Color

If your poster will have color, add _____ to each of the prices above.

Live Performance

You may perform a skit advertising your product at the cost of _____ per airing. Prior to the performance you must obtain the permission (in writing) of the teachers in whose rooms you will air your commercial. Each performance should be between 1 and 2 minutes in length.

Planning Your Advertising

What are the facts you want to tell people about your product? What are the product's strong points? Why would someone want to buy your product? _____

_____

_____

Here is a list of advertising techniques that are often used in print and media advertising. You might want to consider using some of these techniques to advertise your product.

- Personal Benefit - It will make you look younger, feel better, more popular
- Endorsement by a celebrity or expert
- Value - Exceptional quality for the price, reduced price
- Bandwagon - Everyone is buying it, wearing it, or doing it.
- Free Gift

☆ Be ☆ a ☆ Star ☆ with...

Advertising Agreement

The company of _____ agrees to purchase the following

advertising space from _____ for the total cost of $_____.

The price includes the materials for making the following posters and the right to display these

posters on campus for the period of time between _____ and

_____ or the right to perform commercials in the classrooms listed. It is

agreed that the company will collect all posters after the last day of the sale and return them

or will face a fine of _____ for each poster not returned. The rental price will be paid

after the final day of sales.

Quantity	Poster Size	Color or Black & White	Price per poster	Total Price

Live Performances

Arrangements have been made for airing of live commercials in the following rooms.

Room	Teacher	Date and Time	Price

Partners _____   _____

_____   _____

_____   _____

Approved by_____
                        teacher

Loan Application

Business Name _____   Date _____

Partners _____   _____

_____   _____

_____   _____

Product(s) to be manufactured and sold

_____

Marketing Plan - How do you plan to sell your product, to whom will you sell it, and how much do you expect to charge for the product?

_____

_____

Production Costs

    raw materials   _____

    equipment   _____

    utilities   _____

    sales space rent   _____

    advertising   _____

    total costs   _____

Amount of Loan Requested

Production costs   _____

Other Sources of money   _____

Amount of loan needed   _____

Interest

_____ (amount of loan) X _____% (rate) = _____ (interest)

Proposed Collateral

_____

_____

This is a request for a loan in the amount of $_____.

Loan Agreement

Business Name _____   Date _____

This is an agreement to advance the company of _____ a loan in the
amount of $_____. It is agreed that the company will repay the total amount of
the loan plus interest in the amount of $_____ for a total repayment of
$_____. In the event the loan and interest cannot be repaid, the lender will
collect the aforementioned collateral. Payment of the loan is due in full on _____.

Lender _____   Date _____

Partners _____   _____

_____   _____

_____   _____

Loan Agreement

Business Name _____   Date _____

This is an agreement to advance the company of _____ a loan in the
amount of $_____. It is agreed that the company will repay the total amount of
the loan plus interest in the amount of $_____ for a total repayment of
$_____. In the event the loan and interest cannot be repaid, the lender will
collect the aforementioned collateral. Payment of the loan is due in full on _____.

Lender _____   Date _____

Partners _____   _____

_____   _____

_____   _____

Test

Name _____

Match each term on the left with a meaning on the right.

_____ 1. lease   a. person who begins his or her own business

_____ 2. collateral   b. an agreement to rent equipment, land, or buildings

_____ 3. expenses   c. items used to manufacture a product

_____ 4. income   d. people who work for a business

_____ 5. profit   e. money a bank charges for a loan

_____ 6. interest   f. money that is left after paying all expenses

_____ 7. labor   g. expenditures for materials, labor, rent, etc.

_____ 8. investor   h. a person who risks his/her money in a business
                                hoping to make a profit

_____ 9. raw materials   i. revenue earned by a business

_____10. entrepreneur   j. goods offered if a loan cannot be repaid

Choose the answer that best completes the sentence or answers the question.

_____ 1. The system in which individuals are allowed to own a business or produce
         products for a profit is called
         a. communism   c. capitalism
         b. socialism   d. militarism

_____ 2. The money that is needed to begin a business (to buy raw materials and
         rent or buy equipment) is called
         a. profit   c. interest
         b. capital   d. collateral

_____ 3. The person who buys or uses goods or services is a(n)
         a. consumer   c. entrepreneur
         b. loan officer   d. bookkeeper

_____ 4. You own a restaurant. A new dish has been added to the menu. You must
         decide on the price of the new dish. Which of the following would not
         be a factor in your decision?
         a. the cost of the ingredients needed for the dish
         b. the price of the food at other local restaurants
         c. the cost of advertising
         d. the day you will begin serving the new food

_____ 5. You open the first sporting goods store in your small community. Fishing equipment
         is your specialty. You are able to receive high prices for your rods and reels
         because no other store in town sells this type of product. This is an example of:
         a. economic resources   c. monopoly
         b. capital   d. competition

_____ 6. Monica has opened a lemonade stand in her neighborhood. Which of the following would influence Monica's decision about the amount of raw materials to purchase each week?

a. the price of lemonade at a stand 10 miles away

b. the amount of lemons and sugar available at the store

c. the flavor of lemonade sold at a nearby stand

d. the amount of glasses of lemonade she can sell at her price

Answer the following questions.

1. Name two things an effective advertisement should have in it.

_____   _____

2. List four things that are necessary to operate a successful business.

_____   _____

_____   _____

3. How does competition affect the production of a particular product?

_____

_____

4. In a small town, there has been a decrease in sales at the locally-owned grocery store since the large national grocery store has opened. The family-owned grocery store cannot compete with the prices of the large store. What two things could the owner do to attract new customers, avoid losing people who have shopped in his store in the past, and stay in business.

_____

_____

5. A local business has become very successful. The owner would like to open a second branch of his store. List two factors that the owner should investigate in deciding where to locate the new store.

_____   _____

6. You want to open a bakery in your town. Name two things that you would want to consider to make your business a success.

_____   _____

7. Would you want to operate your own business someday? Answer as completely as possible, giving three detailed reasons for your choice.

_____

_____

_____

_____

_____

Answers

Business Vocabulary Answers

boycott - refuse to purchase or use a particular product as a means of protest

budget - a plan to establish expenses

capital - money needed to start a business

capitalism - an economic system in which the businesses are privately owned for profit

collateral - any item(s) of value promised to the bank as payment in case the loan is not completely repaid

consumer - a person who buys services or goods

entrepreneur - a person who begins and operates a business

expenses - the money required to buy materials or cover the costs of a business

free enterprise system - a system in which individuals are permitted to own businesses and use capital to produce goods for a profit

income - money received into a business

interest - a charge for a loan of money, usually a percentage of the amount borrowed

labor - people who work for the business

lease - an agreement to rent a building or land, usually for a specific period of time

loan - a grant of temporary use of money

market - the possible consumers of a particular product

monopoly - exclusive control or ownership of a service or product

profit - money left after all expenses have been paid; income less expenses

raw materials - all things needed to produce a particular product

rent - payment made periodically by a tenant to an owner or landlord in return for use of land, buildings, etc.

retail - the sale of goods to the ultimate customer, usually in smaller quantities (*as opposed to wholesale*)

Test

Matching

1. b	6. e
2. j	7. d
3. g	8. h
4. i	9. c
5. f	10. a

Multiple Choice

1. c	4. d
2. b	5. c
3. a	6. d

Short Answer

Answers will vary but include the following:

1. location, special pricing, times the business is open, goods that are offered for sale

2. good prices, quality merchandise, pleasant, helpful sales staff, merchandise that people want to buy

3. Competition affects the price of a product, quantity produced, and the quality of the product. Generally competition forces retailers to offer better products at cheaper prices.

4. Answers could include free delivery service, extended hours, offering unique products, special ordering products customers want, offering friendly, helpful service.

5. expense of the land or building, competing businesses that are close by, demographics of the surrounding population, availability to existing distribution system, duplicate use of advertising or personnel

6. location, competing businesses, price of raw materials, consumer demand

7. Answers will vary.

Printed in the United States
by Baker & Taylor Publisher Services